A HELEN EXLEY
GIGGLE[...]

Foo[...]

IT DRIVES US[...]

CARTOONS BY BILL STOTT

"Come on lads. I'm keeping
it simple this week..."

"Your million dollar bargain just tied his own bootlaces together."

"Why are we out of the Cup? Well, I think it's because our team's useless and we've scored once in nineteen matches..."

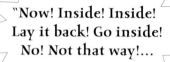

"And from here I can see that Rover's No. 7 isn't happy with that decision..."

"O.K. I want a nice open pattern – Dean and Gary making runs down the flanks, Tommo and Wayne drawing in their defenders. While all this is going on, you Eric, will run about kicking anybody you don't recognize..."

"Look! A sponsor's a sponsor – now put it on!"

"Our Gary's soccer crazy – he's out in the yard trying out his dives..."

"It's that new signing Boss – the chaps are just making sure he knows how to roll about and scream in agony at the slightest contact with an opposing player..."

"False eyelashes may be a first in the world of football face painting, but I'm not sure I want to sit with you..."

"Timbuktu v Outer Mongolia... Oh goody!"

"He's going through his after-goal
crowd adulation response..."

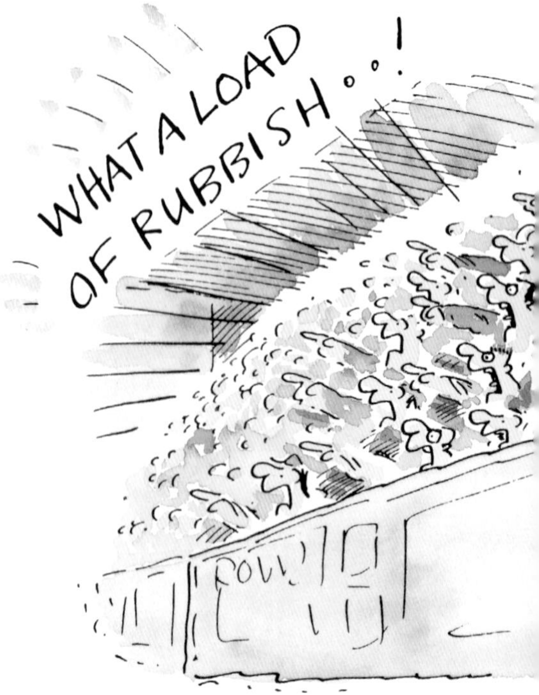
WHAT A LOAD OF RUBBISH...!

"Relax, providing there's no extra time,
we'll make the church, easy!"

1

"Smile...!"

"His dad's very worried about him – he wants a referee's outfit for Christmas!"

"Then Grandad said 'Here's one I bet they don't teach you at school' and kicked it straight through the new window..."

"Well Brian, at the end of the day, the ref's decision is final, despite him being a two-faced, lying rat who's probably on the take."

"Don't tell me. Shanghai v Manila... right?"

"I hate it when the referee is fair
and you **still** get beaten..."

"My Youth Club is organizing a 'Dads' and 'Kids' match. Please, please come and...

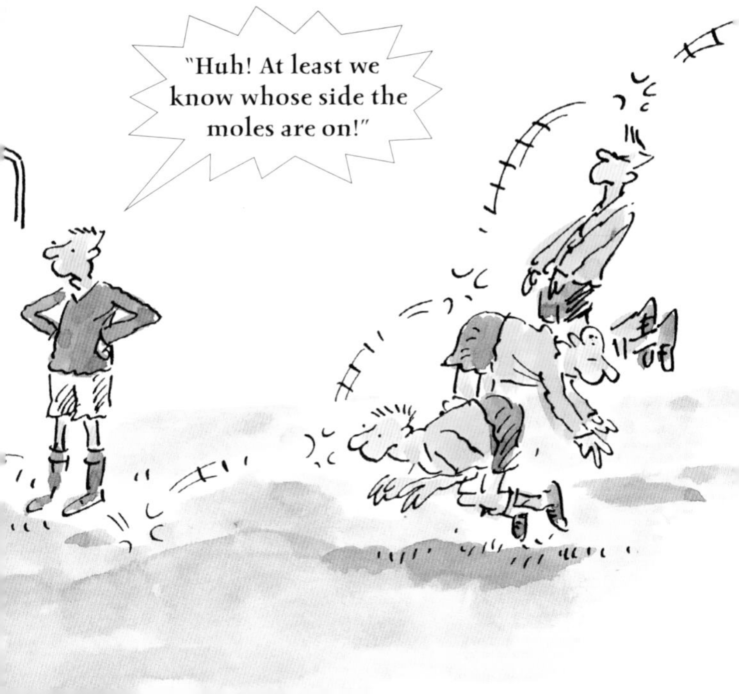
"Huh! At least we know whose side the moles are on!"

2

"Look at that. Not a blink.
 And he knows the score at the end!"

"Isn't that Saturday's ref?"

"They always do that – the only other time
they line up together is to face a free kick..."

"Huh – seven nil. We don't support
our team. We prop them up!"

"Great goal, Gary. Gary? …Where's Gary?"

"I said, 'My mother's coming to stay for a month. The kids have run away and your car's on fire!'"

"Well, we've had a pretty lively debate here tonight..."

"There's a guy in the dugout wants a word
with you. He's a Hollywood talent scout..."

"I don't suppose there's anything in the rules about that, Ref?"

"Huh! They've even got better names than us!"

"Their No. 7 was good, wasn't he?"

About Bill Stott

Bill Stott is a freelance cartoonist whose work never fails to pinpoint the absurd and simply daft moments in our daily lives. Originally Head of Arts faculty at a city high school, Bill launched himself as a freelance cartoonist in 1976. With sales of 2.8 million books with Helen Exley Giftbooks, Bill has an impressive portfolio of 26 published titles, including his very successful *Spread of Over 40's Jokes* and *Triumph of Over 50's Jokes*.

Bill's work appears in many publications and magazines, ranging from the *The Times Educational Supplement* to *Practical Poultry*. An acclaimed after-dinner speaker, Bill subjects his audience to a generous helping of his wit and wisdom, illustrated with cartoons drawn deftly on the spot!

What is a Helen Exley giftbook?

We hope you enjoy *Football – it drives us crazy!*. It's just one of many hilarious cartoon books available from Helen Exley Giftbooks, all of which make special gifts. We try our best to bring you the funniest jokes because we want every book we publish to be great to give, great to receive.

HELEN EXLEY GIFTBOOKS creates gifts for all special occasions – not just birthdays, anniversaries, weddings and Christmas, but for those times when you just want to say 'thanks' or 'I love you'. Why not visit our website, www. helenexleygiftbooks.com, and browse through all our present ideas?

ALSO BY BILL STOTT
Marriage – it drives us crazy!
Cats – they drive us crazy!
Rugby – it drives us crazy!
Sex – it drives us crazy!

Information on all our titles is also available from
Helen Exley Giftbooks, 16 Chalk Hill, Watford WD19 4BG, UK. Tel 01923 250505
Helen Exley Giftbooks, 185 Main Street, Spencer MA 01562, USA. Tel 877 395 3942